Phonicability Games

VERA CONWAY

FOUR-LETTER WORDS

crab

frog

drum

nest

hand

Phonicability Games

CONTENTS

Published by Hopscotch Educational Publishing Ltd,
29 Waterloo Place, Leamington Spa CV32 5LA.
(Tel: 01926 744227)

© 2000 Hopscotch Educational Publishing

Written by Vera Conway
Series design by Blade Communications
Illustrated by Jean de Lemos and Tony O'Donnell
Printed by Clintplan, Southam

ISBN 1-902239-49-0

Introduction

The idea of inventing games of this nature was first conceived out of sheer desperation when I met my first uncooperative pupil. He told me confidently "I do not need to learn to read because I am going to be an actor." As he was then only seven years old and quite unable to project his mind into the future, no argument of mine could convince him to believe otherwise.

A year later when this boy was diagnosed as being severely dyslexic he was triumphant. He stubbornly closed his mind to everyone's attempts to help him and his behaviour in school gave much cause for concern, but our lessons continued. I spent two hours with him each week and, in spite of himself, he learned to read and write. The almost-miracle was achieved by means of games we played together, which he actually enjoyed.

Since then, every game in this series has been played time and time again with pupils who have a variety of problems as well as with those who appear to learn to read and write without experiencing any difficulties. As I saw more and more pupils benefiting from playing the games, I wanted to share them with other pupils – both old and young – so that they could experience the joy and laughter that come with learning to read and spell. I hope, also, that school teachers, parent teachers and helpers of all kinds will become better acquainted with the simple logic of teaching reading and spelling by phonics (sounds).

This is by no means a return to something old-fashioned in a back-to-basics approach. We are all discovering the real worth of a teaching method which, speaking generally, has not been profoundly comprehended. Nor has it been widely appreciated, so the subject could not have been taught effectively in the past. Fortunately, things are changing now; the extensive illiteracy throughout English speaking countries has excited much research. This adds authenticity to many small, enlightening experiments and discoveries currently being made by the few teachers who have the courage to probe. We are finding not only that it is pleasurable to teach reading and spelling by phonics, but also that hardly any pupils need to fail to learn to read.

I use these games in conjunction with Mrs Violet Brand's scheme, using the order in which the sounds are introduced in *Fat Sam* (Egon). Each game supports and extends the new steps within the structure of the scheme, but they can be played in any order.

The games are unbelievably simple and, in principle, well within the capabilities of every potential reader, from the youngest beginners to older pupils who may be experiencing difficulties. Currently, my youngest pupil is five and the oldest is 57! One of my pupils, who was 14 when I first played the games with her, was so impressed by their efficacy that she is now studying child care and working with young children and is designing and making games of her own to help them.

Each game either practises and reinforces the sound/symbol relationship which has just been taught or introduces the pupil to the next one. Some games combine these two aims. When the games are presented to the pupil at the optimum moments in her reading development, newly learned rules are established. (NB We have used 'she' throughout this book to refer to the pupil. This is done purely for the purposes of consistency and clarity. It is not intended to imply that females have more problems with reading than males. In other books in the series we shall use 'he' throughout.)

Although these games can help any pupil to learn to read and spell, they have proved to be particularly useful and effective for pupils who have experienced years of failure in most of their school subjects because of their poor reading skills. One eight-year-old boy who was sent to me to receive 'help' draped himself over the back of his chair as we began the first lesson and refused to look at anything on the table. Learning to read had become anathema to him; he had received plenty of 'help', but he still couldn't read and so he had given up trying. His reaction presented a tense moment for me; I did not know the child and I certainly did not want to spoil our relationship before it had even begun! I took out a game and shook the dice. "Look Perry," I said. "I am playing a game, and I am winning." Fortunately, he won… and gladly came again.

Success in winning the games does not depend on a pupil's ability to read or spell. The real secret of success lies in the fact that, quite subtly, the learning/teaching element is relegated to second place in favour of 'luck'. Because of this, pupils do not feel anxious when they play. There are no worries or tensions; they are confident that they **can** tackle something that appears to be so easy. In such a relaxed atmosphere, they can enjoy the fun of playing and even the triumph of beating the teacher! This latter achievement boosts the confidence of almost every pupil and it is very important to them. I have heard little ones discussing the play later in the day and looking very pleased with themselves as they've said, "I won two games today."

On the other hand, if the pupil loses, she can experience losing a game respectably, without any sense of failure, since she knows that she lost because the dice did not fall in her favour and definitely not because she was stupid!

Teachers will not, of course, be trying to win! On the contrary, and especially with younger pupils or those whose confidence needs to be built up, the teacher will contrive to lose the game! They will soon learn subtle ways to lose, by forgetting where the winning card is, by missing a turn, by always allowing the pupil to go first at the beginning of play, by working out whose will be the last card and by making helpful suggestions to the pupil so that she gets the advantage. I have also even turned a blind eye to a little cheating that works towards my purpose. Pupils have to know what they are doing in order to cheat… but of course I make it very clear that I do not approve of cheating and I correct it when I 'see' it!

Each game has its own very clear aim about which part of the reading structure it supports. There are, however, some subsidiary aims which make the games even more valuable; look out for these as you play.

ASSESSMENT

This is sometimes, for me, the main reason for playing a game. I often need to assess how much of the new work the pupil has assimilated and whether or not she is ready to go on. I assess the situation continually as I watch her strategies as she plays the game. I 'listen' to her thinking processes and to the use she makes of the sounds in the words. I need to know if she is really hearing the sounds or travelling down the dead-end road of remembering the words in 'look and say' fashion. If the latter is true, I know that more practice, more patient explanation and more adaptation to approach the problem from a different angle are all needed. During every game, I have to learn when to wait patiently for the pupil to remember and when to intervene with reassuring help. Playing these games has, in fact, helped me to be able to assess more precisely where my pupil is in her progress and how to help her move on.

VOCABULARY

Each of these games extends the pupils' spoken vocabulary as well as helping them to read and spell. I always talk to them about the words we are using, about the meanings of the words and how they fit into sentences. I have been surprised by the number of pupils who do not know how to use some of the simple, three-letter words such as 'tub', 'wig', 'den' and 'pan', let alone the more difficult ones. I encourage the pupils to give clear definitions of the words to help them to remember when they later need to read them and use them in their own compositions.

MEMORY TRAINING

Memory training is intrinsic to many of the games and with some ingenuity on the part of the teacher even more use can be made of the games to help pupils remember than might at first be apparent. I often ask questions while we are playing, such as "Where is the elephant?" or "Is the stork under the 'ar' or the 'or'?" The most difficult part of learning to spell is remembering which symbol to use from the selection which represent the same sound: 'ai', 'ay', 'a-e' for example. Should 'rain' be spelled 'rane', 'rayne' or 'rain'? The games most certainly help to sort out problems of this kind.

As you become more familiar with the games, countless opportunities will occur to you to use the materials to test pupils' memory skills.

CONCLUSION

It has been my intention to make the games simple, attractive and fun to play. I have borne in mind, too, that they need to be played in a short time because I know from experience how little time many teachers have to spend with individual pupils.

I hope that the games can be photocopied cheaply so that copies may be taken home. Young children especially like to share what they have enjoyed with their families and the additional practice will be good for them. Alternatively, sets of games can be made up and stored as a resource, which can be lent to parents and returned.

The clear aims and simple rules help parents to become effective teachers who, in turn, can give valuable help in playing the games with other pupils. The components of the games may also be used as a resource to illustrate specific teaching points. I have used the games in this way with older pupils who do not necessarily need the competitive approach.

The pictures will also inspire many useful worksheets and ideas for new games, so there are many uses for these photocopiable materials.

PLAYING THE GAMES

Most of the games are designed for two players who can either be the pupil and the teacher or two pupils playing together with the teacher or competent adult as referee. All reading games need supervision and mine are no exception, but the simplicity of these enables parents and classroom helpers to grasp the principles quickly to support the work of the teacher.

The rules of these games are very flexible and can be modified by the teacher to suit the pupil. Pupils sometimes change the rules and I have been happy to allow them to do that provided that the game is still fair and the main aims are accomplished.

There is a great deal of repetition of the rules across the selection of games. This aids each pupil's confidence and allows them to concentrate on the main purpose of the game without having to contend with more complicated instructions.

Pupils should move through the scheme at their own pace and teachers will find that there are more games for those sound/symbol groups, which need most practice. Not all pupils need to play all of the games. Teachers need to be aware of individual pupil's needs. There is little to be gained from playing a game once a pupil has understood that step, except, perhaps, to boost her confidence.

Teachers and helpers need to make sure that pupils know what the pictures represent before the game begins. Such a preview lends opportunity to talk about words and pictures and is an important part of the learning process.

HOW TO MAKE THE GAMES

○ Photocopy the required pages according to the instructions for each game, enlarging or reducing as you prefer. I made all my games to fit into zipped reading book folders measuring 40 x 27cm. This helps to keep the weight down when I have to carry a selection of games to school.

○ Colour the pictures; I have found coloured pencils to be the best tools to use. Enlist the help of anyone who is willing, but if you intend to make your games permanent, make sure that your 'colourers' have high standards.

○ Cut up the sheets as instructed and mount the pieces and the boards on card using an adhesive.

○ If you intend to cover your games with Tacky Back, (and this will certainly preserve them for much use in the future) then use water-based ink pens. Spirit-based ink spreads under Tacky Back. You may prefer to mount the games on thinner card and laminate them.

EXTRA EQUIPMENT REQUIRED

○ Nearly all of the games can be played in a shorter time, if necessary, so I find it useful to carry an egg-timer in my bag.

○ Blank dice can be obtained from:-
Taskmaster Ltd, Morris Road, Leicester LE2 6BR

○ Make your feely bags from attractive pieces of material. Cut out a rectangle which is just a little longer than an A4 sheet of paper. Stitch the sides and hem the top. Thread a string through if you wish.

○ Buttons can be used for counters, or you can buy some from Taskmaster (see previous column). For 'counters' to move on the board, I collect trinkets or small toys from cereal packets. All these little novelties help to make the games more attractive.

○ Stock up with zipped reading book folders for simple storage. I label my folders with my own description of the contents so that I can find the game I need quickly. I also put a mounted copy of the rules for the game into the folder with the pieces.

○ Patience! – You will need much patience too. If you have a will to teach reading, patience grows with the thrill of achievement in both pupil and teacher. I trust that these little games will bring much satisfaction to many people.

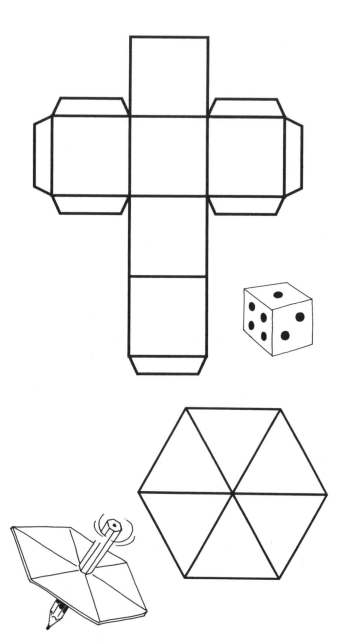

An emergency dice or spinner can be made using the pattern opposite. You can enlarge or reduce it according to your needs.

SOUNDING OUT AND BUILDING
FOUR-LETTER WORDS,
THOSE WITHOUT COMPLICATIONS

Using this Book

REVISION OF THREE-LETTER WORDS

The first four games in this book will help pupils to revise sounding out three-letter words for reading and spelling. They should be able to do this confidently before proceeding to play the four-letter word games.

FOUR-LETTER WORD GAMES

Some pupils need much practice before they can keep four sounds in mind for long enough to produce a word. Often they leave a sound out, saying 'pod' for 'pond'. These games will help draw attention to the importance of every sound in the word.

The games also introduce pupils to the blending of two consonant sounds before or after the vowel sounds. Remember that blending is all-important. The adult should demonstrate to the pupil how to allow the sounds to emerge gently, in succession and in the right order, without adding any other 'rogue' sounds which require an unwanted change in the position of the lips, tongue and teeth. For example,

Mmmm aaaa nnnn (man) and not **muh an ner**

Find the Word

AIMS

○ To give additional practice in hearing, visualising and selecting the correct vowel for a given three-letter word.

○ To help with memory training.

HOW TO MAKE THE GAME

○ Cut up the sheets to make three kinds of squares – words, pictures and vowel sounds. Stick the appropriate vowel sound letter to the back of each word card.

HOW TO PLAY

○ Turn the word cards over so that the vowel sound is facing upwards.

○ Group word cards with same vowel together in an orderly manner.

○ Give each player three picture cards and stack the rest.

○ The first player begins by selecting a word card from one of the vowel groups. She should do this purposefully, having one of her three picture cards in mind.

○ If the card she selects can be paired with her picture, she may set the pair aside as her own and take another picture card from the stack.

○ If she made a wrong choice, she must replace the word card carefully and try to remember not to take it again until she needs it. It will help players to observe each other as they may need the cards that their partners reject. When all the cards have been used up, the winner has the most pairs.

TEACHER GUIDANCE

This game incorporates revision with memory training. It presumes that extensive work has already been done on first sounds and three-letter word building.

Once the game is set up according to the instructions, you may need to help the pupil to decide which of her three words she is going to look for first. Having determined that, ask her which vowel sound she is going to look for. She will then need to read the word she has chosen to see if it pairs with her picture. Do not rush in to help. Give her quiet time to work it out. If she hesitates too long, find out where the problem is. It may be that she is sounding the last letter incorrectly, or she may need lots more practice in building three-letter words. Be sensitive to find out where she is operating.

A note of revision for the teacher – when you need to know how to sound a letter, get your mouth ready to say a word that begins with that letter but do not say the word. Just let that first, tiny sound come out. It will be 'd' not 'duh' or 'der...og...ger' (dog).

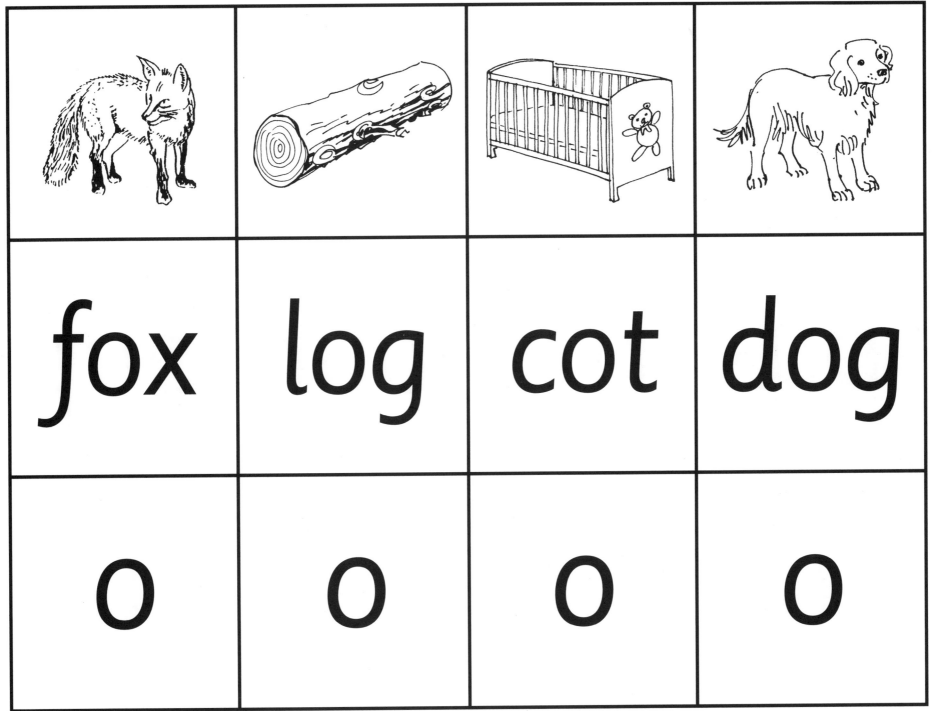

fox	log	cot	dog
o	o	o	o

bus	rug	bun	pup
u	u	u	u

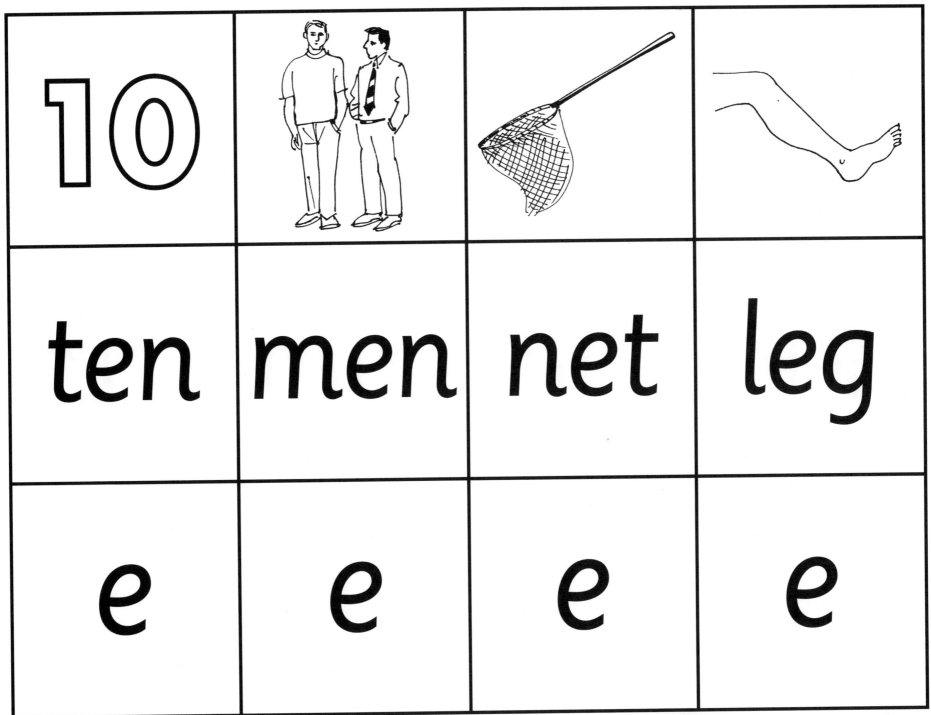

10	ten	men	net	leg
	e	e	e	e

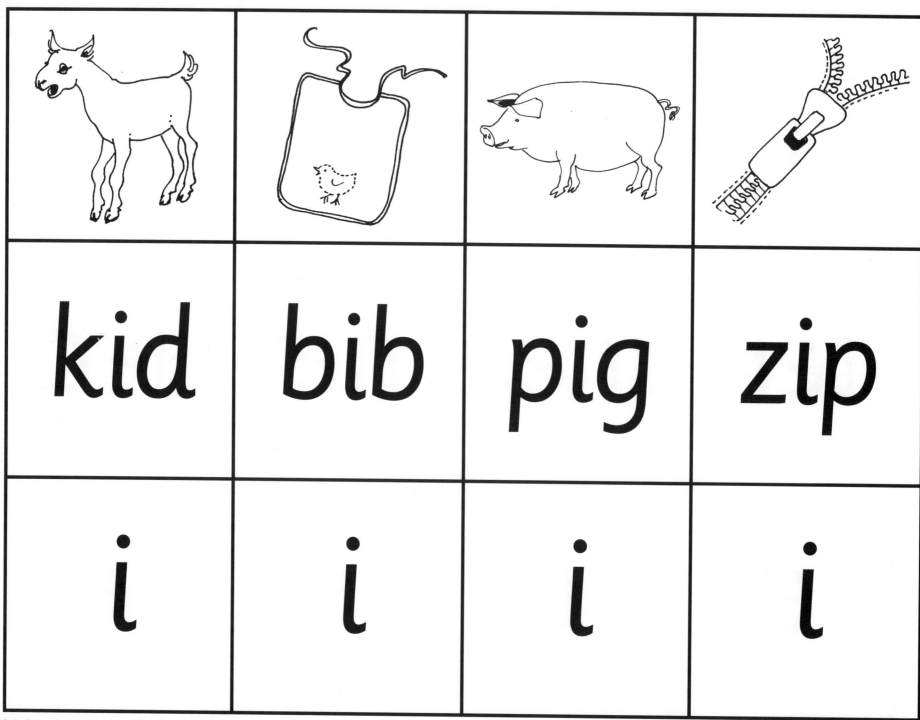

kid	bib	pig	zip
i	i	i	i

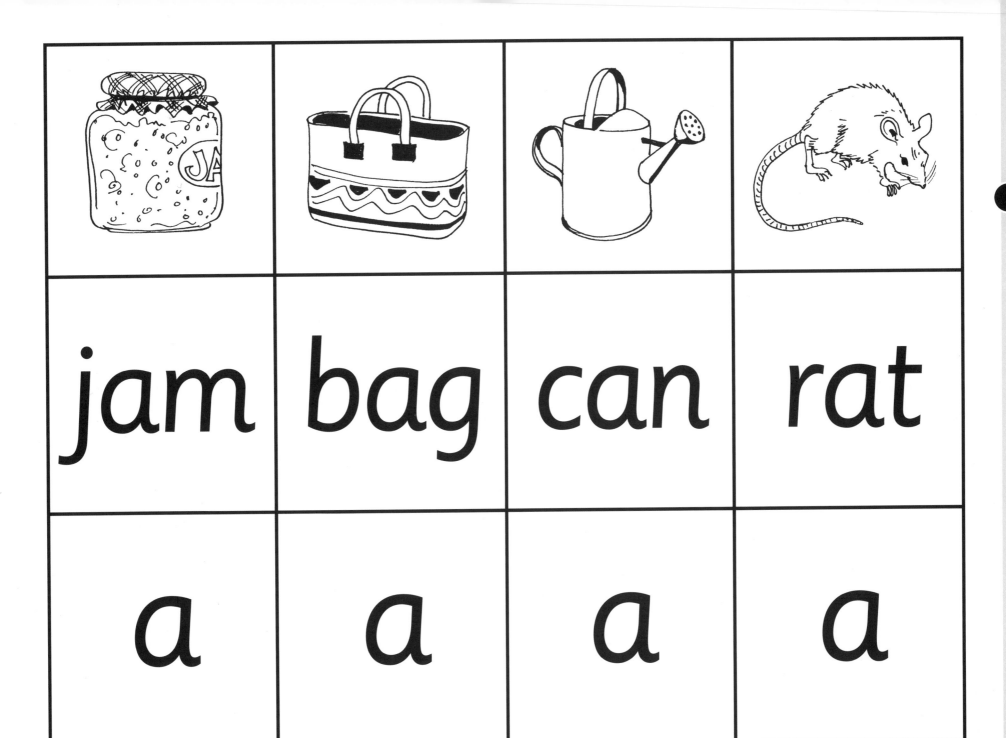

jam	bag	can	rat
a	a	a	a

Speedy Reading and Spelling

SPEEDY READING AIMS

○ To encourage quick recognition of three-letter words without sounding them all out.

○ To give extra practice in using the vowels which the pupil may find most difficult.

SPEEDY SPELLING AIM

○ To help pupils to speed up their sounding out and spelling of the three-letter words.

SPEEDY READING

HOW TO MAKE THE GAME

○ Cut up the picture sheets and separate the small word cards. Sort and store pictures and words in small envelopes labelled with one vowel sound each.

WHAT YOU NEED

○ A dice marked with 1, 1, 2, 2, 3 and 3.

○ A shaking cup.

○ An egg-timer may also be useful.

HOW TO PLAY

○ Choose the vowel sounds that most need to be practised.

○ Spread out the picture cards neatly, picture side up, on the table. Place the word cards, word side up, in groups according to the vowel.

○ Players take turns to throw the dice. They must match as many picture cards and word cards as the number thrown.

○ When the time has ended, or the cards are all used up, the player with the most pairs is the winner.

TEACHER GUIDANCE

Try playing this game by dealing nine or 12 picture cards to each player who must then arrange them neatly in front of her and proceed as above. The first player to cover all her pictures is the winner.

Speedy reading gives more practice to the confident pupil and affords an opportunity to focus on any vowel sound that is still weak. If this game is played with a group, the teacher will need to keep a watchful eye to see that all the matching is correct. The game can be divided to make two smaller sets.

SPEEDY SPELLING

HOW TO MAKE THE GAMES

○ There are two games here. For both games you should cut out all the picture and word cards and affix the appropriate word to the back of each picture card.

WHAT YOU NEED

○ One egg timer.

HOW TO PLAY

GAME 1

○ Scatter the cards, picture side up, over the table.

○ On 'Go', the egg-timer is set and the first player has to choose as many pictures as she can pick up and spell (aloud) correctly before the sand runs through. She may then challenge another pupil.

GAME 2

○ Use the cards in a reading game, by playing in the same way as in Game 1 but spreading out the cards word side up.

TEACHER GUIDANCE

This game is a permanent resident in my schoolbag. It is very useful as part of my assessment equipment when I interview a new pupil and want to find out about her knowledge of word building. It is also useful for demonstrating the value of knowing letter names, but only more able pupils who have understood that letters have names and sounds are allowed to use the names. Do not allow the speedy nature of the spelling to distort the sounds, for example 'buh…in…ner' instead of 'b…i…n'.

These cards are invaluable as a visual aid for adults working with pupils who are learning to build their three-letter words. For example, the pupil can be shown the picture and asked to supply the missing sound when the adult writes '…at'.

box	top	tub	mug
mud	sum	rug	cup
	$$\begin{array}{r} 2 \\ +\,2 \\ \hline 4 \end{array}$$		

jam	cap	mat	hat
pan	van	rat	fan

PHONICABILITY FOUR-LETTER WORDS

wig	cot	pot	mop
log	fox	dog	hot

bin	lid	six	bib
pig	dig	kid	zip

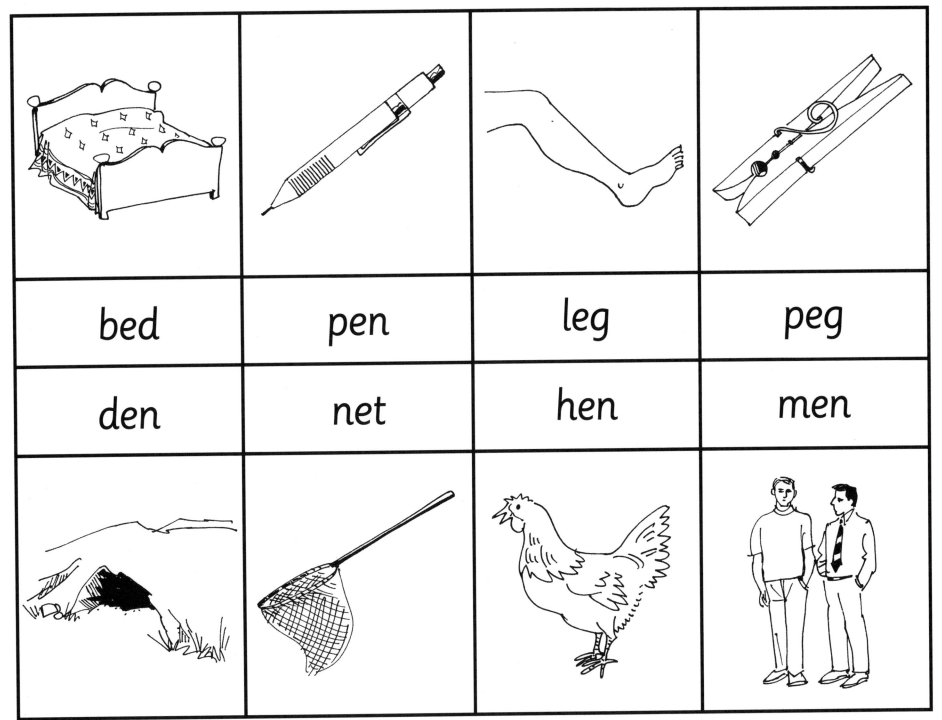

| bed | pen | leg | peg |
| den | net | hen | men |

| bun | bud | nut | jug |
| gum | sun | bus | pup |

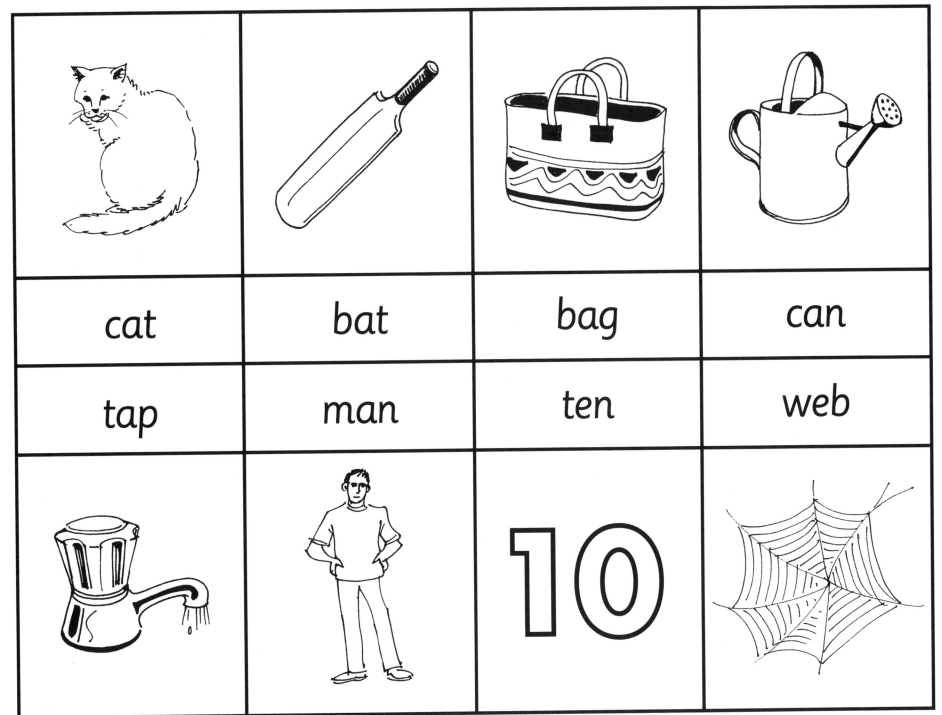

| cat | bat | bag | can |
| tap | man | ten | web |

Smiley Faces
Find the Missing Letter

AIM

○ To help pupils hear the individual sounds in four-letter words and be able to supply the one that is missing.

HOW TO MAKE THE GAME

○ Cut the picture sheets into cards and cut off the letter at the end, as indicated.

WHAT YOU NEED

○ A dice with five smiley faces and one sad face on its sides.

○ A shaking cup.

○ An egg-timer may be useful if you wish to limit the game to a shorter time.

HOW TO PLAY

○ Spread the single letter cards over the table, letter side up, and stack the word/picture cards.

○ Players take turns to throw the dice. If a smiley face is thrown, the player takes a word/picture card from the stack and a letter to fill the gap. If it is the correct letter to finish the word, she keeps the completed word to one side. If it is not correct she returns both to where they were. If a sad face is thrown, she must miss his turn.

○ The winner is the player who has the most completed words when all the cards are used up, or at the end of the preset time.

TEACHER GUIDANCE

Before playing this game with a pupil, choose a group of four-letter words from the game and help her to hear all four sounds in proper sequence. Explain to her that when she plays the game there is one 'sound' missing from the words and, when it is her turn, she must listen to the sounds, then fit the missing one in place.

Watch for pupils trying to supply a sound that is already there – 'vsst' = 'vest'; trying to put a last sound too soon, even though the last sound is already in place – (pmum) plum; not recognising the picture or not knowing the word for it. Hearing those four sounds in sequence takes quite a lot of understanding and practice. Give help if it is needed by saying the sounds in the word clearly and slowly. Let the pupil put her finger under each sound and say it with you till she 'hears' the missing one.

l	l	o	r	n
ag	t	g	ab	d
f	be	fr	c	ha

d r i	p		
r u m	p		
m	l k	i	
n e	t	s	
p l	g u	n	

PHONICABILITY FOUR-LETTER WORDS

p	ot	s	
n	d	sa	
m	p	la	
n	d	po	
c	lip		

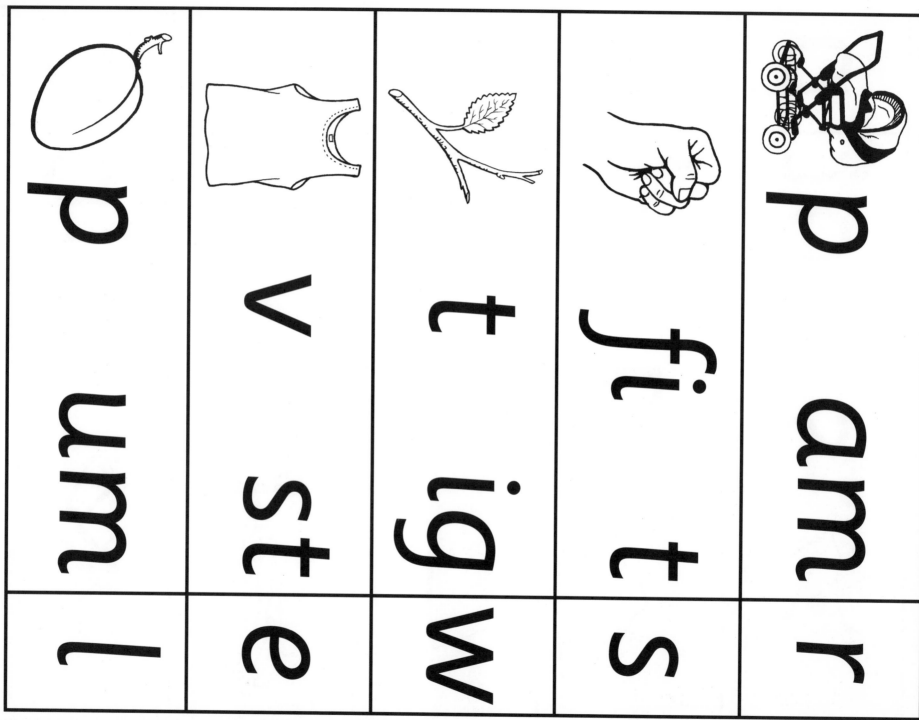

The Box Game
Read and Match Four-Letter Words

AIM

○ To give practice in sounding out and reading four-letter words.

HOW TO MAKE THE GAME

○ Photocopy the word sheet on page 30 twice and cut them up to make small word cards. Place them all word side down in a box with a lid. The picture sheets are the boards.

WHAT YOU NEED

○ It would be helpful, but not absolutely necessary, to have a shallow box (18cm x 14cm x 3cm approx). Alternatively, the cards may be heaped on the table.

HOW TO PLAY

○ Players choose a board each and the small word cards are placed, word side down, in the main part of the box. Players take turns to take a word card from the box. They may keep the word card if it matches a picture on their board. If it does not match they must put it back in the box.

○ If the picture on the board is already covered with a word, the surplus word card should be placed into the lid of the box. (This ensures that, every so often, players miss a turn.)

○ The first player to cover all of her pictures with words is the winner.

TEACHER GUIDANCE

This is a reading game demonstrating four sounds working together to make words. Many pupils find reading easier than spelling, so this game usually gives great satisfaction. The pupil blends the sounds and is able to place the words accurately. Occasionally, pupils misread a word because they only look at the first letter. One might try to put 'frog' on 'flag' or 'plug' on 'plum'. Sound out the whole word and impress on her the importance of every letter.

sand	nest	pond	spot	vest
plug	drip	belt	twig	frog
drum	crab	swim	pram	milk
flag	clip	hand	lamp	plum

Green for Go
Read and Match Four-Letter Words and Pictures

AIM

○ To give practice in reading and matching four-letter words with their pictures.

HOW TO MAKE THE GAME

○ Cut up the picture cards and the small word cards. Stick one of each pair of words on the reverse of the appropriate picture card.

WHAT YOU NEED

○ A dice marked on five sides with a green spot and a red spot on the sixth side.

○ A shaking cup.

HOW TO PLAY

○ The remaining small word cards should be placed neatly, word side up, on the table so that all are visible. The picture cards are stacked, picture side up.

○ Players take turns to throw the dice. If a green spot is thrown, the player may take a picture card and find a word to make a pair. The adult may ask the pupil to spell the word she needs to assess her reasoning. The pupil may check for accuracy by looking at the word on the back of the picture.

○ Words and pictures that have been 'won' may be set aside until all have been used up. The winner is the player with the most pairs.

○ If a red spot is thrown the player must miss a turn.

TEACHER GUIDANCE

Although it is not usually advisable to have more than two children playing a game together, other children often enjoy just watching the play and thus learning from what they see. I played this game on the classroom floor on one wet afternoon, surrounded by a dozen or so keen supporters. "Can I play now, Miss?" they pleaded. Players received better help from their friends than I could give and a great deal of reading and spelling was accomplished. Teachers just need to see that the pairing is accurate and the sounding is careful.

drum	hand	clip	nest	belt
drum	hand	clip	nest	belt
lamp	sand	plug	milk	frog
lamp	sand	plug	milk	frog
flag	plum	fist	pram	skip
flag	plum	fist	pram	skip
drip	vest	twig	spot	crab
drip	vest	twig	spot	crab

PHONICABILITY FOUR-LETTER WORDS

The Sun, Moon and Stars Games

AIMS

○ To give continued practice in reading and matching four-letter words with their pictures.

○ To help sound out and read more quickly four-letter words.

HOW TO MAKE THE GAMES

○ For Game 1 the picture sheets are the boards. Cut up the small word cards and stack them. Cut up the sun, moon and stars cards and place them in a feely bag. (The sun, moon and stars sheet can be copied twice and the symbols stuck back to back to make double-sided cards.)

○ For Game 2 use the picture sheets as boards and cut up the words to make flash cards.

GAME 1

WHAT YOU NEED

○ A feely bag containing the sun, moon and stars cards.

HOW TO PLAY

○ Players may have one or two boards each.

○ The small word cards are placed neatly face up on the table.

○ Players take turns to take a card out of the feely bag. If a star is taken out, the player may take a word card and place it appropriately on her board. If a moon card is drawn, she must miss her go, but if a sun card comes out, then the player may choose two words.

○ The winner's board is filled first.

TEACHER GUIDANCE

This game is for practising the reading of four-letter words. It can be adapted for group play. I have found it very useful to use the same pictures to make several different games. The pupils become comfortable with the familiar. They remember from the 'other game' what the

pictures represent and confusions between 'hand' and 'fist' for example, are already resolved. Familiarity and repetition are assets during this stage of laying firm foundations.

GAME 2

WHAT YOU NEED

○ For up to four players. You will need 24 counters – pebbles or buttons will do.

HOW TO PLAY

○ Players choose one board each and are given six counters. The flash cards are shuffled and stacked.

○ The teacher takes a card from the stack (not necessarily from the top) and holds it up for the pupils to see. The pupil who has the picture to match the word places a counter on the right picture. If the word is not recognised, it should be placed somewhere in the stack to be recycled. The winner is the first player to get six counters on his board.

TEACHER GUIDANCE

Stop the game when someone has won it. Do not continue until one player has 'lost'. Try to match the ability of the players fairly. They will help each other, but one child who knows more than the others could, by telling everyone what the words are, defeat the purpose of the game. I usually advise the players to raise a hand if they own the word. They may read the card aloud if it has been correctly identified.

PHONICABILITY FOUR-LETTER WORDS

PHONICABILITY FOUR-LETTER WORDS

drip	crab	plug
nest	lamp	fist
flag	hand	vest
tent	clip	pond

spot	belt	desk
twig	drum	sand
swim	pram	milk
frog	skip	plum

Watch your Partner
Read and Match Four-letter Words

AIM

○ To practise sounding out and reading four-letter words.

HOW TO MAKE THE GAME

○ The word sheets should be cut up to make small cards and the picture sheets used as boards. A second, similar game may be made by using the word sheets for the boards and cutting up the pictures.

HOW TO PLAY

○ Players choose a board each and the small cards are scattered, face down, over the table.

○ Players take turns to choose a small card. If the picture for that word is on their board, they may place it appropriately. If the word does not match, it should be placed face down on the table.

○ Players should be encouraged to watch each other's play and they should especially watch to see where their partner places her unwanted card on the table.

○ The winner is the first to fill her board.

TEACHER GUIDANCE

I am often surprised by the pleasure and benefit that the pupils obtain from playing the simplest of games. The pupil with whom I play this game soon realises that if I replace a card with a great flourish because I do not need it, then the picture for it must be on her board. She grabs it triumphantly – to find that she has to read it before he can place it. Occasionally my help is needed to sound out a word, but sheer determination to win usually motivates my young partner to read the word carefully.

44

pram	frog	drum	pond
clip	crab	hand	twig
vest	flag	fist	belt

PHONICABILITY FOUR-LETTER WORDS

stag	sand	drip	swim
skip	milk	plum	lamp
desk	nest	spot	plug

Consonant Blends Games

AIMS

○ To help pupils to hear the blending of two consonants at the beginning of words.

CONSONANT BLENDS – GAME 1

HOW TO MAKE THE GAME

○ There are two sheets to make picture boards. Cut up the letter sheets into small cards.

HOW TO PLAY

○ Players choose a board each. The small letter cards are placed neatly, face down, on the table. Players take turns to select a card and place it, if they need it, on one of the pictures on their board. The card is returned to the pool if it cannot be used.

○ The winner is the first player to cover all her pictures with letter cards.

TEACHER GUIDANCE

In the book *Alpha to Omega* by Bev Hornsby and Frula Shear, it is stated that 'since much difficulty is encountered with these blends, much work will be needed on them.' I have found that to be true; some pupils still make the occasional mistake of leaving out one letter of the blend when they are well into their studies. It is important for the teacher to know that these are simply two or more sounds blended together. The sounds retain their individuality – 's' is still 's' and 't' still 't' in 'st'. Pupils only need to be trained to hear the sounds. They do not have, as in the case of 'sh', 'th' and 'ch', a new sound picture to remember. The teacher will need to emphasise the sounds at the beginnings of the appropriate words during the course of play. The sound 'squ' will need a special mention.

CONSONANT BLENDS – GAME 2

HOW TO MAKE THE GAME

○ Cut up both letter and picture sheets into small cards.

HOW TO PLAY

○ Make two stacks of small cards. The first of picture cards face down, the second of letters cards face down. A third stack will be of used letter cards.

○ Each player selects two picture cards and places them on the table in front of her. Players then take turns to take the top card from the letter card stack. If she can pair her letter card with one of her picture cards, she sets the pair aside. She then takes the top card from the picture card stack. If she cannot make a pair with her letter card, she must place it on the stack for used letter cards, letter side up.

○ The next player may take her letter card from the letter card stack or from the used card stack.

○ When all the cards in the letter card stack have been used up, the used letter cards should be shuffled, turned face down and reused in the letter card stack.

○ When all the cards have been used up, the winner will have the most pairs.

TEACHER GUIDANCE

Make sure that the pupil is hearing and saying the blends accurately. Watch for speech problems and work towards correcting them. Do not be concerned about the spelling of the rest of the word, but work towards correct pronunciation. Listen for 'i' in 'slide' – it is not 'sloid'; 'flower', not 'flayer'; 'snail', not 'snayall'.

gr	bl	sw	sc
sm	sk	br	cl
sn	tw	st	sl

br	pl	tr	cl
squ	gl	cr	sp
fr	pr	fl	dr

PHONICABILITY FOUR-LETTER WORDS

Sink the Pirate Ship

AIMS

○ To give pupils practice in sounding out and reading four-letter words quickly and accurately.

HOW TO MAKE THE GAME

○ Make two copies of the picture of the ship – these are the boards.

○ Photocopy the word cards on to card, blue if possible, and cut them up into smaller word cards.

WHAT YOU NEED

○ A dice marked 1, 1, 2, 2, 3 and 3

○ It would be useful to have a bag or box in which to store the word cards while you are playing.

HOW TO PLAY

○ Players take turns to throw the dice and then take that number of word cards from the store.

○ The cards must first be read, then placed anywhere the player chooses on the grid on the ship board.

○ The first player to 'sink her ship', that is to cover her board with words, is the winner.

TEACHER GUIDANCE

Properly, a word card should be replaced in the store if the player cannot read the word correctly. Whether or not I insist on that rule depends on the ability of my pupil. Some who are still struggling to hear the word behind the sounds will really benefit from some help as they play. Be patient and prepared to wait before leaping in too soon. Some pupils stare at a word for what seems to be a long time and you might think they are defeated by it, but they suddenly come up with the right word. They may prefer to do the 'sounding out' silently. I do not press them to do it audibly. I cannot see their thought processes but I know what is going on from what they say as they decode the word. I listen and 'feel' when they need my intervention.

left	fist	snap	crop
silk	clap	fret	next
rust	jump	lamp	test
bump	sand	land	frog
crab	snip	club	melt
bend	golf	film	step

soft	belt	twig	pram
grin	slug	snap	lift
desk	spin	mist	flag
drip	spot	slip	swim
glad	plum	milk	vest
twin	help	trap	drop

PHONICABILITY FOUR-LETTER WORDS